SPOTLIGHT ON GEORGIA

DEVELOPMENTS IN GEORGIA DURING THE LATE 20TH CENTURY

SAM CROMPTON

PowerKiDS press

NEW YORK

Published in 2018 by The Rosen Publishing Group, Inc.
29 East 21st Street, New York, NY 10010

Editor: Elizabeth Krajnik
Book Design: Michael Flynn
Interior Layout: Reann Nye

Photo Credits: Cover Popperfoto/Getty Images; p. 5 Al Stephenson/AP Images; pp. 6, 19 Courtesy of the Library of Congress; p. 7 PhotoQuest/Archive Photos/Getty Images; pp. 9, 11 Hulton Archive/Getty Images; p. 13 Jessica McGowan/Getty Images News/Getty Images; p. 14 SADAYUKI MIKAMI/AP Images; p. 15 Kasuhiro NOGI/AFP/Getty Images; p. 17 Historical/Corbis Historical/Getty Images; p. 21 Tom Hill/WireImage/Getty Images; p. 23 Jemal Countess/Getty Images Entertainment/Getty Images; p. 25 Heritage Images/Hulton Fine Art Collection/Getty Images; p. 26 Henryk Sadura/Shutterstock.com; p. 27 Stephen Morton/Getty Images News/Getty Images; p. 28 Chris McKay/WireImage/Getty Images; p. 29 Marcus Ingram/WireImage/Getty Images.

Cataloging-in-Publication Data

Names: Crompton, Sam.
Title: Developments in Georgia during the late 20th century / Sam Crompton.
Description: New York : PowerKids Press, 2018. | Series: Spotlight on Georgia | Includes index.
Identifiers: ISBN 9781508160069 (pbk.) | ISBN 9781508160090 (library bound) | ISBN 9781508160076 (6 pack)
Subjects: LCSH: Georgia--Juvenile literature.
Classification: LCC F286.3 C76 2018 | DDC 975.8--dc23

Manufactured in the United States of America

CPSIA Compliance Information: Batch #BS17PK For further information contact Rosen Publishing, New York, New York at 1-800-237-9932.

CONTENTS

CHAPTER ONE

COMING OUT OF THE CIVIL RIGHTS MOVEMENT

The passing of the Civil Rights Act of 1964 and the Voting Rights Act of 1965 marked two major victories for the civil rights movement. However, this didn't mean the struggle for equality was over for African Americans in Georgia. Violence against African Americans was still a big problem well into the late 20th century. In rural areas of the state, African Americans didn't experience as many benefits from the civil rights movement's victories.

As years went by, schools became more **integrated** and **segregation** lessened. New people in Georgia's government and the federal government in Washington, D.C., brought more positive changes. As a result, Georgia's economy began to boom toward the end of the 20th century and the beginning of the 21st century. Today, Georgia's economy flourishes because of the tourism, film, and shipping industries. Cities such as Savannah and Atlanta are important centers of global **commerce**.

In 1980, less than 10 percent of elected state officials were black. In 1973, Maynard Jackson won the election and became Atlanta's first African American mayor. He was the first African American mayor of a major southern city.

CHAPTER TWO

A SMALL-TOWN GEORGIA BOY

Jimmy Carter is one of the most **influential** people to come from Georgia. James Earl Carter Jr. was born on October 1, 1924, at a hospital in Plains, Georgia. He was the first future U.S. president to be born in a hospital. His father was a well-known peanut farmer, and his mother worked as a nurse before Carter was born. When Carter was a boy, the family lived in a home that didn't have electricity or indoor plumbing, just like many other homes in the area at that time.

CARTER'S CHILDHOOD HOME

Jimmy Carter graduated from the Naval Academy in 1946. He was in the top 10 percent of his class. After graduating, Carter went to work on submarines in the U.S. Navy.

Carter graduated from high school at the top of his class. He was the first person from his father's side of the family to graduate at all. Carter attended two Georgia colleges before beginning his studies at the U.S. Naval Academy in Annapolis, Maryland.

CHAPTER THREE

THE CARTERS MOVE BACK TO GEORGIA

After years in the navy, Carter left the military and moved back to Georgia in 1954 with his wife, Rosalynn, and their children. Carter's father had died in 1953, and his mother needed him on the family farm. However, there was a terrible period of very little rain that year and the business suffered because of it.

That same year, the Supreme Court declared segregation in schools unconstitutional in the *Brown v. Board of Education* decision. This case marked the beginning of many changes in the South. In 1955, Carter was elected to the Sumter County Board of Education. Many southerners were against integrating public places. Carter was the only white man in Plains who refused to join the segregationist group called the White Citizens' Council.

Carter held leadership roles in other areas besides education, too. These roles allowed him to become more involved and better known in his community.

Jimmy Carter helped keep the family peanut farm up and running. Carter's hard work and management skills made the farm prosperous by 1959.

CHAPTER FOUR

MAKING CHANGES IN THE SOUTH

Carter's father had been serving in the Georgia state legislature at the time of his death. Carter also wished to serve his community in this way. In 1962, a seat opened up in the Georgia State Senate, and Carter decided to run for it now that the family business was stable.

Carter ran against Homer Moore, a local businessman. At first, the vote showed Moore won the race, but Carter suspected Moore of cheating. Carter appealed his loss and a Georgia judge declared Carter the rightful winner. During his two terms as a state senator, Carter became known for his support of civil rights and his efforts to fight wasteful government spending practices. Although he fought for the continued integration of schools, Carter's peers voted against his proposals. Working toward changes in education was at the core of Carter's position as a state legislator.

During Carter's time as a Georgia state senator, he proved that he was **dedicated** to serving the people of Georgia.

CHAPTER FIVE

A FAILED FIRST ATTEMPT

Carter ran for the position of Georgia governor in 1966. The election happened shortly after the Civil Rights Act and the Voting Rights Act were passed, and many people in Georgia reacted to these advancements in civil rights by voting for politicians who didn't support them. Carter's opinions about civil rights didn't help him in the race. He ended up in third place. The new governor of Georgia, Lester Maddox, was a noted segregationist.

In 1970, Carter ran for governor again. His campaign this time around focused on rural white voters who hadn't voted for him the first time. He took a step back from many civil rights issues. It worked: Carter was elected as Georgia's 76th governor in 1970.

While in office, Carter fought against segregation and for advancements in civil rights. He reorganized the state government and focused on the state's education system.

Carter's grandson, senator Jason Carter, has followed in his grandfather's footsteps. He ran for the position of Georgia governor in 2014.

CHAPTER SIX

MAYNARD JACKSON MAKES A DIFFERENCE

In 1973, during Jimmy Carter's term as Georgia's governor, Maynard Jackson was elected mayor of Atlanta, Georgia's capital city. One of Jackson's largest concerns while in office was working toward equality for the city's **minority** population. He worked hard to make sure that minority workers had a fair chance at jobs and that minority-owned businesses had equal opportunities to get government contracts.

Maynard Jackson (left) shakes hands with Juan Antonio Samaranch (right), president of the International Olympic Committee, after Atlanta won the bid to host the 1996 Summer Olympics.

In 1990, during Jackson's third term as Atlanta's mayor, Atlanta was chosen to host the 1996 Summer Olympics. The Olympic flag was passed to Jackson at the conclusion of the 1992 Olympics in Barcelona, Spain.

During his first two terms as mayor, Jackson also focused on dealing with police violence toward African Americans. Crime rates fell, but a string of murders terrorized the city from 1979 to 1981. Jackson worked to keep the city calm.

Jackson could only serve two terms in a row as mayor, so he convinced his friend Andrew Young to run for mayor in 1981. In 1989, Jackson ran for and won a third term.

CHAPTER SEVEN

CARTER FOR PRESIDENT

After his success in Georgia's capital, Carter decided to run for the office of U.S. president in 1976. Carter's determination and previous government experience helped him during his campaign. Carter was an ideal candidate for many voters simply because he hadn't been involved in the federal government and wasn't connected with issues such as the Vietnam War. Carter won the election and took office on January 20, 1977.

During his single term as president, Carter had to deal with many issues left over from Presidents Richard Nixon and Gerald Ford. In the 1970s, problems with oil supplies caused gas shortages and drove up the price of gasoline. Unemployment was a serious issue, and the United States' economy was suffering. Each of these issues combined to create what some people called "stagflation"—a **stagnant** economy paired with ever-increasing **inflation**. President Carter did his best, but problems continued.

The Panama Canal Treaty of 1977 was one of President Carter's greatest achievements while in office. This treaty settled problems between the United States and Panama over control of the canal.

CHAPTER EIGHT

YOUNG FILLS JACKSON'S SHOES

Andrew Young was elected Atlanta's mayor in the 1981 election, following Maynard Jackson. Before he was elected, Young was a pastor at a church in Thomasville, Georgia. He devoted himself to civil rights **advocacy**. In 1961, Young started working with the Southern Christian Leadership Conference in Atlanta. This civil rights organization, led by Martin Luther King Jr., helped register thousands of rural African Americans to vote. Young was with King when the civil rights leader from Georgia was killed in 1968 in Memphis, Tennessee.

Young was elected to the U.S. House of Representatives in 1972. He and Barbara Jordan from Texas were two of the first black southerners to be elected to Congress in the 20th century. Continuing his civil rights advocacy, Young supported the poor and working-class citizens of America. His efforts caught the attention of President Carter, who named him ambassador to the United Nations in 1977.

Young's work as the United States ambassador to the United Nations focused on developing countries and the fight for basic human rights.

When Young became mayor of Atlanta in 1981, it marked the first time that two African Americans in a row had been the mayors of a major southern city. During his time as mayor, Young worked hard to create new jobs and businesses and was reelected in 1985. He had an enormous role in the campaign for Atlanta to host the 1996 Summer Olympics.

Young decided to run for the position of Georgia governor in 1990 but was defeated. Young created the Andrew Young Foundation, which supports education, human rights, and more, in 2003.

Young's influence made a difference in many Georgians' lives. A number of places bear his name, including Morehouse College's Andrew Young Center for International Studies and Georgia State University's Andrew Young School of Policy Studies.

Young received the Presidential Medal of Freedom from President Jimmy Carter in 1981.

CHAPTER NINE

AFTER THE PRESIDENCY

Jimmy Carter ran for president again in 1980 but lost. He and his family returned to Georgia. Carter and his wife, Rosalynn, founded the Carter Center in Atlanta in 1982. The Carter Center works with Emory University to help people in countries around the world. As part of the center's activities, Carter visited Cuba in 2002. He was the first former or current president to do so since Calvin Coolidge visited in 1928. During his visit, Carter made several **diplomatic** appearances and spoke on Cuban television.

Carter received the Nobel Peace Prize in 2002 for his dedication to international peacemaking. Carter was the third president to receive the award—Presidents Theodore Roosevelt and Woodrow Wilson were the first and second. The only other native Georgian to receive this honor was Martin Luther King Jr. The University of Georgia presented the Carters with the Delta Prize for Global Understanding in 1999.

Carter has written 29 books and was accepted into the Georgia Writers Hall of Fame in 2006. He is a two-time Grammy Award winner for the best spoken word album.

CHAPTER TEN

THE OLYMPICS COME TO ATLANTA

When Andrew Young and other Georgia leaders bid for Atlanta to host the 1996 Summer Olympics, they promoted it as a city that boasted the best of the South and an up-and-coming center of economic development. After the International Olympic Committee announced that Atlanta would host the 1996 Summer Olympics, work began on the Olympic village and other structures.

It took a lot of work to prepare Atlanta for the Olympics. However, many of these improvements and new buildings benefited the city during and after the Olympics. The city added valuable hotel space, improved roads and sidewalks, and beautified the city with greenery and new works of art. All of these efforts cost about $5.14 billion and took six years to complete. However, Atlanta was now positioned as a city involved in the global economy.

The Olympics boosted Atlanta's tourism industry. People from across the country and around the world came to see the city.

CHAPTER ELEVEN

EXPANDING SAVANNAH'S HARBOR

The city of Savannah and its port have played an important role in Georgia's economy for hundreds of years. In 2015, Savannah's harbor included the United States' fourth-busiest container port. There, containers are taken off cargo ships and put onto other ships, trains, or trucks.

The Savannah Harbor Expansion Project, which began in 2015, will make the harbor and the Savannah River deeper so that more ships–and bigger ships–can use the port. An expansion project completed at the Panama Canal in 2016

In 2002, colonial-era remains were found near the site of the Savannah River expansion project. The remains were part of a trading post located at the site in the 1700s and 1800s.

means that bigger ships carrying more goods will be arriving at U.S. ports. The Georgia Ports Authority estimates that the project will create over 350,000 jobs, which will boost Savannah's economy.

Expanding Savannah's harbor will cost about $706 million. It took the Georgia Ports Authority over 15 years to plan this project, which is expected to bring $174 million to the U.S. economy.

CHAPTER TWELVE

GEORGIA'S FILM INDUSTRY

Georgia's **diverse** landscape, mild weather, and efficient transportation have made it an ideal location for the film industry. Since the 1970s, hundreds of movies, TV shows, and commercials have been shot in Georgia. The highest grossing movie filmed in Georgia is *Hunger Games: Catching Fire*, which made $425 million in the United States.

HUNGER GAMES FAN EVENT
ATLANTA, GEORGIA

The film industry also contributes to Georgia's booming tourist economy. Some towns in which films or TV shows have been shot are now tourist attractions. Covington, Georgia, features tours for *The Vampire Diaries* and *The Originals* fans. Juliette, Georgia, is a tourist attraction for fans of the movie *Fried Green Tomatoes*.

Georgia legislators have encouraged filmmakers to film in Georgia by providing tax credits to film companies. Since the mid-2000s, these tax credits have helped bring more filmmakers to Georgia and made more money for the state.

The Atlanta Film Festival, which takes place every year, shows documentaries, short films, and feature-length films from around the world. The Plaza Theatre, shown here, is Atlanta's oldest operating and only independent cinema. It opened in 1939.

CHAPTER THIRTEEN

LOOKING TO THE FUTURE

Georgia's economy and political environments greatly improved throughout the late 20th and early 21st centuries. Jimmy Carter made changes in Georgia and the United States starting from his time on the Sumter County Board of Education. Carter continues to work toward bettering people's lives through the Carter Center.

Maynard Jackson and Andrew Young helped diversify Atlanta's leadership. They fought to help African Americans in the city by creating new jobs and challenging police brutality. They also helped Georgia gain global recognition through hosting the 1996 Summer Olympics in Atlanta.

In more recent years, Georgia has actively sought a share in the global economy. The Savannah Harbor Expansion Project is expected to create thousands of new jobs and contribute to Savannah's economy. The film industry in Georgia draws tourists from around the world, positively impacting Georgia's economy. In the next few decades, Georgia may continue to experience economic and political growth.

GLOSSARY

advocacy (AD-vuh-kuh-see) The action of supporting a cause.

commerce (KAH-mers) The large-scale buying and selling of goods and services.

dedicated (DEH-dih-kayt-ed) Having very strong support for or loyalty to a person, group, or cause.

diplomatic (dih-pluh-MA-tik) Having to do with handling relations between one's country and other countries.

diverse (dy-VERS) Made up of things that are different from each other.

inflation (in-FLAY-shun) A sharp increase in the price of goods, sometimes caused by a shortage of goods.

influential (in-floo-ENT-shul) Having the power to cause change.

integrated (IN-tuh-gray-ted) Allowing all types of people to participate or be included.

minority (muh-NOR-uh-tee) A group of people who are different from the larger group in a country or other area in some way, such as race or religion.

segregation (seh-gruh-GAY-shun) The separation of people based on race, class, or ethnicity.

stagnant (STAG-nent) Not active, changing, or progressing.

INDEX

PRIMARY SOURCE LIST

Page 6
Jimmy Carter's childhood home in Plains, Georgia. Photograph. Now kept at the Library of Congress Prints and Photographs Division, Washington, D.C.

Page 17
Jimmy Carter and General Omar Torrijos shake hands after signing the Panama Canal Treaty. Photograph. Created September 7, 1977, by White House staff photographers. Now held by the National Archives and Records Administration.

Page 19
Andrew Young at a meeting of the Subcommittee on African Affairs of the Senate Committee on Foreign Relations. Photograph. Created June 6, 1977, by Thomas J. O'Holloran. Now kept at the Library of Congress Prints and Photographs Division, Washington, D.C.

WEBSITES

Due to the changing nature of Internet links, PowerKids Press has developed an online list of websites related to the subject of this book. This site is updated regularly. Please use this link to access the list: www.powerkidslinks.com/sog/20cent